The Rule-Free Golf Swing

Improve your game with four simple pictures

Chris Riddoch

Copyright © Chris Riddoch, 2017
www.thegolfswingzone.com

Published by Chris Riddoch, 2017.

The right of Chris Riddoch to be identified as the Author of the Work has been asserted by him in accordance with the Copyright, Designs and Patents Act 1988.

All rights reserved.

Golf swing image drawings by Richard Nordström.
Cover image by Richard Nordström.

This book is sold subject to the condition it shall not, by way of trade or otherwise, be circulated in any form or by any means, electronic or otherwise without the publisher's prior consent.

Contents

INTRODUCTION 1

1. A BRIEF HISTORY OF SKILL 3
  THE PROBLEM WITH MECHANICS 3
  HOW WE DEVELOP SKILL 4
  THE POWER OF IMAGES 7

2. SWING IMAGES 9
  IMAGE 1: THE CLOCK FACE 11
  IMAGE 2: THE BALL ON A ROPE 13
  IMAGE 3: THE CORKSCREW 15
  IMAGE 4: THE FISHING ROD 17
  IMAGE 5: THE PERFECT SHOT 19

3. LOOSE ENDS 21
  THE LITTLE SWINGS 21
  PRACTICE 22
  THE GOOD PLAYER 23

SUMMARY 25

ABOUT THE AUTHOR 26

INDEX 27

INTRODUCTION

In 2012, I published *The Golf Swing: it's easier than you think*, the first book to describe scientifically the simplest and most effective way to improve a golf swing. The book described a new approach based on the principles of *motor skill science* rather than the traditional swing mechanics approach. Since publication, I've had many requests to translate the science into a guide explaining what players actually need to *do* when they practise and play.

This book is that guide. It's short – you'll probably read it in comfortably less than an hour – and there's a reason: improving a golf swing isn't complicated. In the time it takes to drink a few cups of coffee, you'll have all the tools you need to make real progress with your swing. This may surprise you because it sounds too simple, but it's fully supported by modern science. It may also surprise you to hear that the traditional approach to swing improvement – trying to move through a series of specific angles and positions – has no basis in science. Or, to give it due credit, it's based on the wrong science.

This is why we feel overwhelmed by complex swing mechanics, confused by swing theories and frustrated by our lack of progress. We practise hard, but nothing seems to work, and we get the distinct feeling we're wasting our time. As one eminent psychologist noted:

> *"Most of the practice most people do, most of the time, be it in the pursuit of learning the guitar or improving their golf game, yields almost no effect."*
>
> —Gary Marcus, Professor of Psychology, New York University.[1]

---

[1] Marcus, G. Guitar Zero—the new musician and the science of learning. Penguin Group, 2012.

But there's a solution—we can switch sciences. We can switch to motor skill science, which shows us how to improve our *skill*. And that's the main point: working on mechanics has little effect on skill; to improve skill, we need to work on skill! When we do this, our swing mechanics fall into place in the way that suits us best – we don't force them into someone else's idea of 'perfect.'

In this book, you'll find a simple, effective approach to improving your skill. You'll start to engage your powerful, innate skill-learning system—the system you stifle when you follow mechanical rules. It's an approach based on images, not words, which your brain will find easier to process. It's your way to a *Rule-Free Golf Swing*.

The book is organised roughly into two parts. First, we'll cover some basic principles of motor skill science to see why it's the simplest and best way to improve a golf swing. Then we'll find out how to use it—what we actually need to do during practice and play. Along the way, we'll strip the swing down to its four essential movements and see how a few carefully chosen images will help us master them. We'll also consider our short game, the best way to practise, how to transfer our new-found skills to the course and how players of all levels can benefit.

So let's start. First, we'll go back to where everything went wrong.

Working on mechanics has little effect on skill; to improve skill, we need to work on skill

---

1. A BRIEF HISTORY OF SKILL

We're only on page three, and we've mentioned the word 'skill' 10 times. And that's the point; the golf swing is a *skill*. To improve our skill we need to understand how the brain learns, remembers and instructs the body to perform the movements necessary to produce a good shot. Note that skill resides in our brain, not our body. Our brain is in charge. Every shot we hit, every good shot and every bad shot, we control with our brain.

Golf, unfortunately, seems to have forgotten about the brain and rushed headlong down a path that focuses exclusively on the body. Now, we know every movement the body makes when it swings a club – in minute detail – but we know nothing about how to make those movements happen. We've put the dumb cart before the intelligent horse.

Our aim is to get the horse back in front. We need to base our swing improvement efforts around our brain's capacity to learn, not around how our body moves. We'll start with where the horse got left behind—when swing mechanics took over.

The problem with mechanics

Sometime back in history, 'golf,' in its desire to make learning and improving the golf swing more scientific, chose the wrong science; it chose mechanics. And now, we're swamped by mechanics. Every year sees dozens of new books, thousands of magazine articles and millions of words describing how our body parts need to move when we swing a club. But the point is: the swing isn't a mechanical problem—it's a skill problem.

But, for whatever reason, we love our mechanics. We can see them, photograph them, analyse them, compare them, copy them and wrap them up in jargon. But unfortunately, swing mechanics only tell us *what happens* during a swing; they tell us nothing about *how to make it happen.* This approach presumes that if we 'perfect' our mechanics we'll improve our skill. Unfortunately, this is wrong. We'll improve a bit because we're hitting lots of balls, but it's a slow, tedious and frustrating process. The hard fact is: there's little relationship between mechanics and skill.

We might also consider today's top players, who produce fantastic performances using swings developed through a mechanical approach. But these players are highly driven, have a huge work ethic and hit hundreds of balls a day. It's their job. The sheer volume of balls they hit is probably enough to compensate for the fact that they're working against their natural instincts. Also, they all swing differently, which suggests they've each found their own best way of swinging, despite their efforts to swing 'perfectly.'

In this book, we'll improve our skill using the principles of motor skill science. We'll get our brain and body working together subconsciously to produce skilful movements. We'll use few words and no mechanical rules. We'll change the swing from a complex movement problem to a straightforward skill problem.

> *"It looks like an octopus falling out of a tree."*
>
> —David Feherty describing Jim Furyck's golf swing.[2]

Swing mechanics only tell us *what happens* during a swing; they tell us nothing about *how to make it happen.*

How we develop skill

If we were machines or robots, the mechanical, rule-based approach to swing improvement would work well. But we're not, so it doesn't. Unlike machines, we don't have rigid levers and fixed joints that perform one simple task unthinkingly over and over again. No, we have floppy bodies consisting of hundreds of stretchy muscles, highly

---

[2] Jim Furyk on Feherty: *The man with the octopus golf swing opens up*, 2014.

manoeuvrable joints, limbs that can move in almost any direction and a complex brain controlling it all. More rag doll than robot. Trying to get this loose, undisciplined body to move unerringly through a long series of highly specific angles and positions is close to impossible. To get it to replicate those movements time after time is totally impossible.

What's happened is this. Evolution, working with our rag doll body, developed a way of learning skills totally devoid of mechanical rules. So we've never developed any mental capacity to convert verbal or written rules into skill. If we try, we're working against millions of years of evolution. It's no wonder we struggle. Mechanical swing rules are, to borrow a phrase from Geoffrey Pullum, Professor of Linguistics at Edinburgh University (and keyboard player in the 1960s band Geno Washington & The Ram Jam Band): "*Zombie rules—though dead, they shamble mindlessly on.*"[3]

Our way forward is to improve our skill in the way evolution intended. We need to train the skill-learning system we *do* have, and it may surprise you to find out what it is—it's our rag doll floppiness. Far from being a hindrance, our flexible, adaptable, highly manoeuvrable body *is* our skill-learning system. That disobedient floppiness we curse during practice is our greatest golf swing weapon – we just need to allow it to work in the way evolution intended. Here's why.

When we make a swing, our body, controlled by our brain, makes hundreds of small, subtle movements involving dozens of muscles. The movements are so subtle and numerous, they're totally beyond our conscious control. However, this doesn't matter because we have a highly sophisticated, *subconscious* control system to do the job. The system is self-correcting; we can swing in many ways and still control the thing that matters most—the club head. We're not aware of it because it's outside our consciousness, but it's immensely powerful. Today's top players have better-trained control systems; they don't necessarily have better mechanics.

Here's the point: to improve our swing, we need to train this subconscious system by allowing it to operate *freely*. It learns by *exploring* different movement solutions to the challenge of hitting the ball; our task is to give it this freedom to explore. When we do this, our golf club control system improves through 'learning by doing,'

---

[3] Pullum, G. *Rules that eat your brain.* Lingua Franca , 2012.

not by being told what to do.

The important thing is to allow our subconscious mind to control the swing, but this won't happen if we allow our conscious mind to interfere. Unfortunately, our conscious mind – our thoughts – will *always* dominate our subconscious mind, so the trick in the golf swing is to keep them as far apart as possible. While our subconscious mind is producing the swing, our conscious thoughts must be on something else—we must banish all thoughts of hands, arms, legs, hips, shoulder turns, weight shifts, angles and positions.

Unfortunately, most of us think of these all the time. Whether we're practising or playing, we consciously try to force our body to do what 'we' want, blindly following the swing rules. We never allow our brain and body to cooperate and work things out for themselves. This is hugely important, and it sends us a key message: we need to stop thinking about how we're moving! Before we find out what we should be thinking about, we need some scientific proof that we're on the right track. Here it is.

In 2014, scientists reviewed 80 high-quality studies that compared an *internal focus* (thinking about body angles, positions and movements) with an *external focus* (thinking about anything except the body) across a broad range of sport skills. Not a single study found in favour of an internal focus; an internal focus was no more effective than telling players: "Just do the best you can." An external focus was more effective in improving players' balance, accuracy, precision, muscular efficiency, force production, speed, coordination and, most importantly, the quality of the skill produced. The results were consistent across 20 sports and were the same in novices, intermediates and experts and in men, women and children. In golf, results were equally strong for the full swing, pitch, chip and putt. Also, players who used an external focus performed consistently better under pressure.[4]

We don't need to labour the point; the results speak for themselves. The rules of swing mechanics, because they force us to focus on our body, should not be used directly to improve our skill. We need an external focus, outside our body, but which is the best? We'll go there next, after I've told you about my bad back.

---

[4] Wulf, G. Attentional focus and motor learning: a review of 15 years. *International Review of Sport and Exercise Psychology* 6,1 77-104, 2013.

"Keep your eye on the place aimed at and your hand will fetch it; think of your hand and you will likely miss..."

—William James, the 'Father of Psychology.'[5]

Our golf club control system improves through 'learning by doing,' not by being told what to do.

The power of images

I have a bad back. I also like to go for walks, and I've been told that I walk with bad posture and this makes my back problem worse. Recently, I decided to improve my walking posture, so I checked out some reliable physiotherapy websites for advice. I found plenty; here's what I need to do:

> 'Look forwards not down; focus on a spot 6–9 metres in front; keep my chin parallel to the ground; tighten my stomach, side and lower back muscles; keep my pelvis horizontal; nod my head slightly; strike the ground with my heel, then roll onto my toes; keep my elbows bent; swing my arms from the shoulders not the elbows; hold my natural spinal curves.'

It was impossible—too many rules. I felt and looked like Robocop. Thankfully, a physical therapist saved me when he said: "Imagine your head is tied to the clouds by a string." This simple image worked perfectly; all the walking rules just fell into place.

This is how we've evolved to learn skills—we use images of what we want to *achieve*, then we just have a go. Let me show you. Try the following test:

1. Place the tip of one forefinger on your knee.
2. Close your eyes.
3. Move your fingertip in a straight line to the tip of your nose.

---

[5] "James, W. *The Principles of Psychology, Vol. 1.* Henry Holt, 1890.

You probably did this well, certainly after a few attempts. Now do it again, this time noting what you think about while you're moving your fingertip. What did you think about? You almost certainly thought about the straight line between your knee and your nose—what you wanted to achieve. Or you may just have thought about your nose—the target.

Now try it a third time, this time thinking about how you rotate your shoulder, bend your elbow, swivel your wrist and stretch your finger. It's difficult to even start, isn't it? You've just discovered that the best way to improve a skill is to think about the result and let your subconscious control system sort out how to do it. No thoughts of angles, positions or movements—just an image of the straight line between your knee and nose.

Focusing on an image of something unrelated to our body and how it's moving achieves the two things we want in every swing: 1) our conscious mind is occupied and can't think about how we're moving and 2) we produce our best, *automated* swing. Put simply: when we think about our movements, we block our automated swing – which is always our best swing – and instead produce a hesitant, jerky, swing-by-numbers. When we think about an external image, we release our automated swing.

This is the big – but only – change we need to make. Rather than approaching the swing as a long series of fixed angles and positions, we focus on images that will make good things happen in our swing. And it's a good swap because we'll be letting go of dozens of position-based thoughts and replacing them with only a handful of images. Life will become simpler.

The best way to improve a skill is to think about the result and let your subconscious control system sort out how to do it.

---

2. SWING IMAGES

I need to come clean; I owe swing mechanics an apology. I've been a bit tough, so I need to set the record straight—swing mechanics are an important part of improving a golf swing. They tell us what should happen in an effective swing, they identify a player's swing faults and they provide the information coaches need to give effective feedback.

The problem is: they shouldn't be used for teaching and learning—they need translating into something simpler that our brain can digest. Enter motor skill science—our translator. Take a look at the following figure.

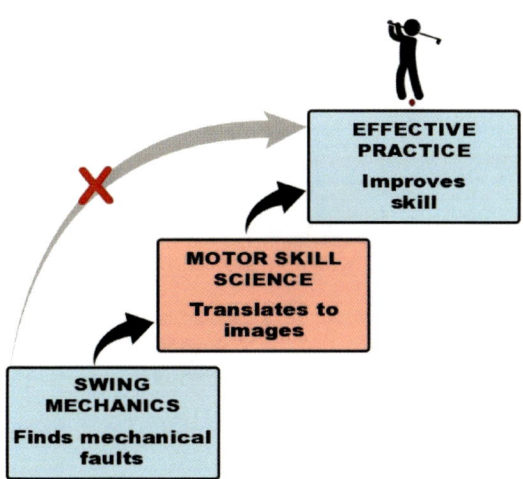

You can see how it works: swing mechanics identify a fault, motor skill science translates it into an image and our brain uses the image to work out the best movements. Anyone who follows the grey arrow and tries to feed raw mechanics directly to the brain will struggle.

This section is organized according to the above figure. We'll use swing mechanics to identify the swing's four *movement fundamentals*: an accurate club head path through impact, a passive wrist release, a well-coordinated muscular chain and a tight initial downswing radius.[6] Then, we'll create an image for each. Don't worry if the fundamentals sound a bit jargonistic; they're actually quite easy to understand.

Our first image is a clock face.

---

[6] For more detailed discussion of these movement fundamentals, including the background science, see Riddoch C. *The Golf Swing: it's easier than you think* (2012).

Image 1: The clock face

Swing mechanics tell us the club needs to travel on the correct plane through the impact zone. The correct plane is the plane on which we held the club at address – the plane the club was designed for. This is our first swing fundamental. To master it, we'll use an image of a clock face – or at least, the bottom half of a clock face.

As we can see, the clock face is lying on its side and leaning towards us; it represents the correct plane through the impact zone. The ball is at 6 o'clock. As we make the downswing, we focus on the clock face and manoeuvre our club so the shaft slides over the clock face's top surface. Simple and effective. Try a few 'air' swings now, and see how it feels.

You can use a whole clock face if you wish, which may help you keep your club close to the correct plane throughout the swing. You may recall that Ben Hogan used something similar: he used to imagine a pane of glass with its bottom edge resting on the ground, just behind the ball, and its top edge resting on his shoulders. He tried to keep his swing underneath the glass.

This would work well, but the best way to develop a skillful swing is to allow it some freedom to wander. If we try to tell it where to go from start to finish, we restrict it too much. It's better to let it roam a little, 'rounding it up' onto the half clock face for the final path through the impact zone.

Image 2: The ball on a rope

Here, we imagine we're swinging a heavy ball attached by a rope to a short grip. This promotes a *passive wrist release* during the downswing, which ensures we apply no 'hitting' force to the club. This is swing fundamental two. It's important because a passive wrist release achieves two things: high club head speed and a square club face at impact.

It works like this. At the midpoint of our downswing, the centrifugal forces in our rotating body force our hinged wrists to unhinge naturally, slinging the club head outwards at great speed. This causes a massive club head acceleration to well in excess of 100 mph at impact in good players. The key word is *naturally*; we mustn't try to make it happen. Any attempt to apply extra force to the club with our wrists or hands will destroy the system.[7]

When swinging a ball on a rope, the only way to get the ball to accelerate powerfully onto the target is to use a slinging, not a hitting, action—just like a golf club.

---

[7] The system is known as a double pendulum.

A brief note

We'll pause here to take stock. We can create an excellent swing if we develop just these two fundamentals. A club swinging through the impact zone on the correct plane, with its club head speeding through via a passive wrist release, gets us an effective swing. And we only have two simple images to think about!

As we progress with these two images, our swing will find its own best movement pattern. Our brain will learn through exploration what works and what doesn't. Gradually, our swing will settle into a more consistent movement pattern that delivers the result we want, and the *motor plan*[8] for these movements will be filed away safely in our brain, ready to be released automatically whenever we need it. This will be our unique, effective swing—our 'swing signature.'

At this point, our swing will be effective but will lack power, so it's important when we practise that we don't expect the effortless power we see in top players. It's also important not to try to inject power—that comes next. Just make easy swings and check how the clock face and ball on a rope improve your club–ball contact and shot accuracy.

Our next task is to inject power, and for this, we need a corkscrew and a fishing rod.

---

[8] A *motor plan* is a package of signals sent from the brain to the muscles telling them how to move.

Image 3: The corkscrew

During the downswing, we imagine we're screwing our body into the ground like a corkscrew, producing muscular force from the ground up. The key phrase is 'from the ground up' because our aim is to create a *coordinated muscular chain*[9] of effort starting with our legs, working upwards through our body and ending up in our arms. This is swing fundamental three.

To produce muscular force while maintaining control of our swing, we must avoid making a maximal effort with just one set of muscles and concentrate instead on *coordination*. Our aim is to generate a series of coordinated muscular efforts through a chain of muscles involving our legs, hips, torso and shoulders. In a well-coordinated chain, each link generates a small amount of force and passes it on to the next link. This link accepts it, adds a small force of its own and passes everything on. This continues up the chain. No link dominates, and force flows smoothly upwards through our body, increasing with each step.

Most of us have enough muscular strength to generate the force

---

[9] Technically known as a *kinetic chain*.

required to hit the ball a long way. Our problem is we let it 'leak out' because our muscles work in the wrong order. We have an *un*coordinated chain. The corkscrew image improves coordination and prevents leaks.

Next, we need to go fishing.

Just before we do, a note for wine-lovers. Those with long experience of uncorking wine bottles will notice two things: 1) for a right-handed player, the downswing is an *un*screwing action; 2) when we use a corkscrew, we apply force to the handle at the top end not the pointy end at the bottom. These are both true, but it's such a good image that we'll call the discrepancies golfing 'artistic licence.'

Image 4: The fishing rod

Image four – our final practice image – simply makes sure we don't waste image three. Image three gets us halfway to effortless power by helping us generate rotational muscular force, but we need to convert that force into *speed*. It's speed that really counts when the club head meets the ball.

The process of converting force into speed is simple—we need to make our body as 'thin' as possible during the first half of the downswing. This is our fourth and final swing fundamental, and it's where the fishing rod comes in. As we start the downswing, we imagine we're holding a flexible fishing rod that wraps itself tightly around our body. This helps us achieve a tight *swing radius*,[10] which creates low swing resistance and hence greater swing speed. Here's how it works.

When we apply a force to an object to make it rotate, a smaller object will rotate faster than a larger object. Not small and large as in terms of weight, but in terms of size and shape. If an object has lots of parts sticking-out – in our case, two arms and a club – this increases

---

[10] The swing radius is the distance between your sternum (centre of your chest) and the club head.

rotational resistance,[11] which slows everything down. So the thinner we can make ourselves, the less resistance we create and the faster we rotate.

We can see this principle at work in the high-board diver who needs to perform three somersaults before they hit the water. They generate rotational force when they jump off the board, then they tuck in their arms and legs as tightly as possible. This reduces rotational resistance and they somersault faster. As they approach the water, they come out of the tuck into an extended position, which increases resistance, slows down their final somersault, and they enter the water vertically.

In golf, when we tuck our arms and club in tight, we prevent another leak—this time a speed leak.

We now have everything we need to improve our swing, but there's a final twist: we need to transfer our practice range swing to the course. The question is: what's the best image to use when we *play?*

---

[11] Known scientifically as the *moment of inertia*.

Image 5: The perfect shot

This is our playing or competitive image—the perfect shot. As we go through our pre-shot routine, we allow an image of the shot to develop in our mind. We see the ball's trajectory, shape, distance, landing point, bounce and roll. We allow the image to develop gradually, so it's clearest while we're making our swing. But why an image of the perfect shot?

When we play and compete, we need to get all four fundamentals to work *in the same swing*, but we can't think of all four practice images in the same swing. So when we play, we can only rely on the *automaticity* we've achieved through practice. We need an image that keeps our conscious thoughts away from our subconscious swing, and our practice images are designed to do just that. We could therefore use one of those, but the perfect shot has some advantages.

Many top players favour the perfect shot image because it achieves two things. First, it stops our conscious mind from thinking about our body movements. Second, because we're 'seeing' the perfect result, our subconscious mind, which needs to put together a motor plan to trigger an effective swing, knows exactly what's needed—it can 'see' the perfect result. So it puts together the best plan – the thousands of subtle muscular movements that will deliver the club head to the ball in a way that produces the perfect shot.

There's another way in which the perfect shot is our best image. We saw earlier that an external (outside the body) focus improves our performance, but remarkably, the *farther away from our body* we can focus our attention, the better our performance becomes. Researchers at the University of Arizona studied baseball hitters and compared the effects of focusing attention on 1) the hands, 2) the bat and 3) the flight of the ball after it's been struck. From worst to best, the results were hands, bat, ball flight.[12]

So here's a little experiment. Below, you'll find 10 external images that all work well, starting with images close to the body then moving farther away. Try them, and see which work best for you.

1. The club head path
2. Perfect ball–club contact
3. The first few metres of ball flight
4. The full ball flight (like you see on TV)
5. The landing area
6. The flag
7. The perfect shot (in its entirety)
8. A target in the sky, e.g. a small cloud
9. The moon
10. Outer space

Or, as in the baseball study, simply compare the effects of focusing on your hands, club and ball flight.

Swing mechanics identify a weakness, motor skill science translates it into an image and our brain uses this to work out the best movements.

---

[12] Castaneda, B & Gray R. Effects of focus of attention on baseball batting performance in players of differing skill levels. *J. Sport Exerc. Psychol.* 60-77 (2007).

3. Loose ends

We've finished, at least in terms of improving our golf swing skill, but we need to tie up some loose ends: 1) how do we use the images for performing golf's other swings – the pitch, chip and putt? 2) what's the best way to organise practice? 3) How can I use this book if I'm already a good player? We'll see.

The little swings

The principles and methods we've discussed don't change for the short game – the pitch, chip or putt. We can use the same images, but we only need the first two because we don't need to generate much force or speed. And for putting, we can forget about all four!

For pitches and chips, we can base our practice on the clock face and the ball on a rope. There are a huge variety of pitch and chip shots, but they all demand two things: an accurate club head path through impact and passive wrists. Hitting shots of varying distances using these two images will improve both accuracy and precision.

The putt is probably the simplest movement in sport, so we have little need for swing development. Despite the huge variety of putting techniques on display among top players, we can be sure of one thing: if one technique was better than the rest, the rest would disappear. It's like diet books: if one worked, the rest would die out. But putting is important, so we need to take a closer look.

As with the full swing, we need to improve our skill, and as we know, we won't achieve this by restricting our mechanics. The fact is, almost identical levels of putting accuracy can be achieved by a range of body movements and swing patterns. Good putters have one thing in common: however they swing the putter, they deliver the putter head accurately to the ball. They've trained their control system, not perfected their mechanics.[13]

To improve our putting skill, we only need one image—the perfect putt. This applies to both practice and play. There's really no better advice than to follow the Jack Nicklaus method: see a movie of the ball rolling across the green and into the hole; then just make it happen.

Practice

Without practice, this book won't work. Most of us set aside time for practice, but we need to use it effectively. We're in a great position to do this because we only have a handful of images to work on; our only task is to work on them in a logical order.

You will have your own way of organising practice, so we won't be too specific, but bear in mind the following:

- The clock face and ball on a rope work together and form the basis of an effective swing. Work on these first, individually to start with, then combine the two. Hit smooth, easy shots with no attempt to generate power.
- The corkscrew and fishing rod also go together and add the power, so these come next. Again, work on them individually, then combine the two.
- Don't try to combine all four! Thinking about four images in one swing is impossible!

You've now given your four fundamentals a good workout, and they'll be more automated, so we could leave it at that. But if we do, we'll be neglecting a crucial practice element: practising to compete.

Spending hours on swing development – even using images – will make us experts, but only 'practice experts.' After we've worked on the practice range, we have a fiendishly difficult golf course to negotiate, so we need to devote part of every practice session to competition-proofing our skills.

We can do this by hitting shots using only our competitive image

---

[13] For more in-depth discussion of putting science and practice methods, see Riddoch C. *Expert Putting: the science behind the stroke. 2013.*

– the perfect shot. To refine our competitive skills even more, we can do it in a way that mimics the competitive situation. We can't mimic it perfectly, but we can come close by doing the following:

- Just hit shots. Use only the perfect shot image. Rely completely on your automated swing. Use different clubs in random order. If you can, find different lies and slopes. Hit half and three-quarter shots. Hit high and low shots. Shape shots. Attempt shots you find difficult. Put yourself under pressure.[14]

This is a crucial part of practice. As one wise coach once said to me: "There's no point in practising practising."

The good player

Players of all levels will benefit from the simpler approach we've outlined. Beginners will clearly benefit from having less to think about, but what about intermediates and experts who already have reasonable swings? Well, they have just as much – maybe more – to gain because the principles of improving a skill don't change with performance level—the best way to improve a skill is *always* the best way to improve a skill.

If you're a good player, you'll benefit from trusting the sound mechanics you obviously already have and allowing your swing some freedom to explore. We say that a wandering, exploring swing has high *variability*. Each swing we make is different from the previous swing. Removing restrictions – not imposing more – increases swing variability and effectively trains the control system. Swing mechanics automatically mould themselves into an individual, effective pattern that suits a player's age, gender, talent, body shape, fitness, mental abilities and even personality. Let me convince you.

Scientific studies consistently show two groups of players have high swing variability: beginners and experts. With beginners, it's easy to understand because they swing all over the place with little control. They clearly have high variability. With the experts, it's the opposite;

---

[14] For more in-depth discussion of effective practice, see Riddoch C. *Winning at Sport: science, skill and the new psychology of outstanding performance.* 2016.

they've found a way to allow their swings to vary, taking full advantage of their powerful, innate control systems.

This explains why so many intermediates don't progress to higher levels. They've become intermediates by taming – restricting – their wild-swinging beginner movements and achieving some control. They're happy with this, but then they make a huge mistake. Because they've improved to this point by restricting their movements, they presume the way to further improvement is to make even more restrictions. They try to reduce their variability as much as possible – ideally to zero. At this point, they believe they'll have the mechanically 'perfect,' fully repeating swing. They're wrong; these players stagnate, becoming the 'perpetual intermediate.'

So here's the advice for better players:

1. Give your swing the freedom to explore its limits.
2. Train your system; don't tinker with mechanics.
3. Don't practise swings—hit shots.

SUMMARY

That's it! You now have everything you need to make real improvements to your swing, and you have the full power of motor skill science behind you. It's not a quick fix. The images are not tips that will work the first time you try them. Nor are they some wondrous new discovery or breakthrough; we've simply applied the correct scientific principles to improving the golf swing. All we're doing is bringing our practice and playing methods up-to-date. We've fixed golf's big problem, at least in our little world.

Let me finish with an anecdote and a warning. In the five years since publication of *The Golf Swing*, I've received hundreds of messages from players and coaches. Most were complimentary, but a few were critical. And here's the thing: the criticisms were always the same—the book was too simple.

So here's the warning: some players like to think of the swing as highly mechanical, technical and complex. They love the swing theories, high-tech equipment and pseudoscientific jargon. They'll tell you about their latest tips, game-changing articles, books and videos. They'll engage you in technical swing discussions at every opportunity. There's no harm in this, and in some ways it's what makes the golfing world go round. So please join in. But when you've escaped, come back to your simple images.

Practise, improve your skill—and enjoy your golf!

"How can you think and hit at the same time?"

—Yogi Berra, legendary baseball player and coach.

ABOUT THE AUTHOR

Professor Chris Riddoch was born in Chester, UK, in 1949. He was a scratch golfer in his teens and represented his college (Borough Road) and county (Cheshire). He had two international trials for England (overlooked, alas). He has degrees in Physical Education and Sport Science and a PhD in Sport Physiology. Chris has worked at the universities of Bath, Bristol, Middlesex and Queen's, Belfast and has published over 200 scientific articles on sport and exercise science. He lives in Stockholm, Sweden, with his wife Maya.

Other books

Winning at Sport: Science, Skill and the New Psychology of Outstanding Performance (2016)
Expert Putting: The Science Behind the Stroke (2013)
The Golf Swing: It's Easier Than You Think (2012)

www.thegolfswingzone.com

INDEX

conscious mind 6, 19
diving, and rotational resistance 18
double pendulum *13n*
evolution, and skill-learning 5
Feherty, David 4
focus of attention
   baseball hitters 20, *20n*
   distance from body 20, *20n*
   external 6, *6n*, 20
   internal 6, *6n*
   test 20
Furyck, Jim 4
Hogan, Ben, pane of glass 11
images
   ball on a rope 13–14
   clock face 11–12
   competition-proofing 22–3
   competitive image (see images: perfect shot)
   corkscrew 15–16
   fishing rod 17–18
   perfect shot 19
   target 8
   test 7
   walking 7
kinetic chain *15n*
learning by doing 5
Marcus, Professor Gary 1
moment of inertia *18n*
motor plan 14, 19
motor skill science 2, 9, *9f*
movement fundamentals 10
muscular chain 15
muscular force 13
Nicklaus, Jack 22
passive wrist release 13
players, level
   beginners 23
   intermediates 23–4
   experts 23–4
   'perpetual intermediate' 24
practice
   competition-proofing 22–3
   effective *9f*, 22–3,
   mimicking competition 22–3
   organising 22–3
   'practice experts' 22
   to compete 22–3
Pullum, Professor Geoffrey 5
rotational resistance 18
self-correcting swing 5
short game 21–2
skill
   control system 5, 21
   history of 3–6
   rag doll, body as 5
subconscious mind 19
swing
   automated 23

beginners v experts 23–4
mechanics 3, 9–10, *9f,* 23
plane 11
radius 17, *17n*
rules 6
signature 14
speed 17
variability 23–4